With grateful thanks,
to all those friends who gave encouragement,
and shared anecdotes of their grandparents
and great-grandparents, and generously gave
their old family recipes, without leaving out
that one important ingredient!
and to my sons who didn't want to hear about
it, till it was finished!
and to the librarians at The Maryland Room,
Enoch Pratt Free Library Maryland Historical
Society, Peale Museum, Baltimore County
Public Library,
again, thank you!

1

This should not be regarded as a serious cook-book for serious cooks, but as a light hearted bouquet garnis of cooking with an historic glimpse at the Inner Harbor of Baltimore.

I will not dwell on ragouts or roasts
Albeit all history attests
That happiness for man, the hungry sinner
Since Eve ate apple, much depends on dinner.

Lord Byron
(1788—1824)

Written and compiled by
Juliette Palmer-Frederick

Drawings by Virginia C. Poetzsch
and Juliette Palmer-Frederick

Copyright © 1984 by Juliette Palmer-Frederick

ISBN 0-89709-139-6

Distributed by:
Liberty Publishing Company, Inc.
50 Scott Adam Road
Cockeysville, Maryland 21030

Lancaster St. Fells Pt.

he Otterbein Church. Cor. W. Conway St. & Sharp St. Sth Balto.
1785-86

The **Old Otterbein Church** was named after its pastor, Philip Wilhelm Otterbein who was the pastor from 1774 until his death in 1813. The building as you see it today, was erected in 1885 and is the oldest church continually used for worship, in Baltimore. It began as a German Evangelical Reformed Church, which in 1800 became the United Brethren Church. Then in 1946 there was a merger with the Evangelical Church, making it the Evangelical United Brethren Church. After the merger in 1969 with the Methodist Church, it became the United Methodist Church, and so it remains today. It is open for worship on Sundays for 11:00 a.m. service. It stands on the corner of Sharp Street and Conway Street just a short walk from the Harbor Place.

CONTENTS

Gaslight. Otterbein

A BRIEF HISTORY OF THE INNER HARBOR

To say the Inner Harbor is steeped in history may be a cliche, but it is true. We walk where not only the founders of Maryland have walked, but the founders of the United States. We tread the path of those settlers, colonists, heroes, artists, inventors, poets, authors, freedom fighters, villains and knaves, all fortunate enough to have shared in the making of this historic city — this place of monuments — this dream of a man, the friend of Kings, whose thoughts on tolerance were the basis for the religious freedom he so meticulously documented, to be carried out in Maryland.

This man, George Calvert, was greatly trusted, first by King James I and then his son King Charles I of England. The King honored him by making him Lord Baron of Baltimore, with the accompanying lands in Ireland, and titles to be passed on to his heirs. George Calvert, like many business men of the time, became interested in the planting of colonies in America, and visited Virginia. He saw the beauty and potential in the lands north of Virginia and requested a grant of land which the *"Most Serene King out of his own noble disposition recently in the month of June 1632, gave this Province to the Lord Baron of Baltimore and his Heirs forever"*.

Owing to his father's death, Cecilius, George Calvert's son, became Absolute Lord and Proprietary of the Province of Maryland, the Lord Baron of Baltimore, and responsible for the planting of Maryland (so named in honor of Charles I wife, Queen Henrietta Mary) and all at twenty-seven years of age; an onerous task at any age. After having made great preparations to go out to the colony, his private affairs and State matters in England, made it impracticable for him to leave. He then commissioned his brother, Leonard Calvert (making him, "Lieut. General, Chief Governor, Chancellor, Commander Captain, Magistrate and Keeper of the Great Seal") to accompany the colonists and establish Maryland.

The Inner Harbor
Baltimore.

Since the founding of Baltimore in 1729, this hill has been a popular place to view the city. An observatory built there in 1795 signalled city merchants of the approach of their vessels. This service lasted for 100 years. The hill was mined for clay and sand, then during the Civil War, Union troops fortified the 'Hill'. It is honey-combed with tunnels and storage areas, which caused many problems in recent years from cave-ins and slides which threatened the 'Hill's' existence. The loss of such a beloved landmark is unthinkable. Many charmingly restored houses are to be found in the streets around the 'Hill'.

8

Federal Hill named May, 1788. Celebrations took place when the Constitution was ratified and a parade of mechanics and merchants marched from Philpott's Hill to Fell's Point, displaying banners which reflected the enthusiastic mood and hope for better days to come. The hoped for protection from foreign trade was noted by the silversmiths, whose banner stated "NO IMPORTATIONS AND WE SHALL LIVE!" (The same slogan heard today, and not just from silversmiths!)

The procession ended at Federal Hill, the site named in honor of the occasion, where the marchers were seated at a circular table "*of 3,600 feet and treated to an elegently disposed repast consisting of 50 Gammons of bacon, as many Rounds of Beef, bbls. of Countrey Beer etc. the whole prepared as a Cold Collation*".

9

Maryland has always been aware of the greater
world outside her borders. She is fortunate
that the blood of her people has been renewed with
the strains of English, French, Irish and German.
Greater tolerance is one of the traits distinguish-
ing the people of Maryland from their neighbor,
Virginia. Tolerance and tobacco were both
cultivated in Maryland. As long as tobacco was
the only export, a town was hardly needed. The
tobacco hogsheads could be rolled down to the
shore anywhere and loaded aboard ship. (Which
is why Rolling Road was so named.) By 1675,
Charles Calvert, the third Baron, had succeeded
to the title. Claims and counter claims concerning
the boundaries of Pennsylvania and Maryland set
out in the charter, continued for many years;
during the Civil War in England and the reign of
Charles II . . . . . . then the flight of James II
and the accession of William and Mary to the
throne of England; the authority of the
Proprietary of Maryland, was not restored until
1716.

An agreement between Charles, the fifth Lord
Baltimore and the sons of William Penn, was
ingeniously worded and mapped incorrectly so
as to deceive Charles. By accepting this agreement, he surrendered everything for which his
grandfather had so vigorously fought.

Although Baltimore was laid out in 1729, it
hardly grew. Twenty years later, there were
only about twenty-five houses. Few ships used
the "Branch". An early sketch shows the site to
have considerable beauty, lying at the foot of
the Piedmont Hills. The town site was shaped
roughly like an 'Irish Harp'. Two of the little
streets that formed it, Uhler's Alley and
McLennan's Alley, meandered through down-
town Baltimore. The straight side of the 'harp'
was formed by a precipice over-hanging the
stream known as Jones Falls, named for David
Jones who was the first settler. It was not really
a falls, only a tumbling stream. *"As is usual in
Village settlements it was thought necessary to
proscribe the geese and swine from running at
large"*. . . . It was also decided, after some time,

to erect a fence which divided the city at Light St. and those using the road were required to pay a toll in order to maintain the road. However, it also became necessary to provide a guard to protect the fence from local residents, who continually took the wood for their fireplaces. The maintenance of the fence became so costly, it was ultimately abolished.

This new town, by the name of Baltimore, was laid out upon Indian River, which empties into the Atlantic. In 1745, Major Thomas Sheridan, Dr. G. Buchanan, Captain Darby Lux and Messrs. Thomas Harrison and William Fell were appointed commissioners, the first two being then, delegates, with John Paca and John Hall Esqrs. Captain Lux commanded a ship in the London trade as early as 1733; in 1743 he purchased Lots 43 and 44 on the west side of Light St. where he resided and transacted much business.

Light St. stretches at right angles to Pratt St. It was here that the steamboat wharves stood. Time was when whole squadrons of little side wheelers would proceed down the river with much froth and fuss, and not much speed, to explore the picturesque features of the Bay. The great delights of these journeys can only be imagined today.

The Harbor is bounded on the north side by Pratt St. a typical waterfront, with warehouses, sailors' hotels and ships' chandlers. The glory which once was afloat, the graceful clippers, Chesapeake Bay rig, log canoes, bug-eyes or pungies with flipper bows and raking masts, the clipper ships which carried the fame of Baltimore throughout the world, are gone.

Sadly, as happens in other cities, no effort was made to protect the beauty or preserve the natural wonders which prompted Father Andrew White, S.J. to write, as he sailed into the Bay, *"This bay is the most delightful water I ever saw between two sweete landes . . . . . . This is the sweetest and greatest river I have seene so that the Thames is but a little finger to it"*. Chesapeake Bay has changed from sail and steamboat country to power boat country.

On the south side of the harbor there were no wharves. There was no room for them, because on this side, facing the town there rises a sheer hill named in 1788, Federal Hill. It has fortunately been kept as a charming, green oasis from which to view the city.

The first open market house was opened in 1763 at the corner of Baltimore and Gay Sts. In 1784 others were opened at Hanover St., Harrison St. and at Fell's Pt. William Speer had the town's first bakery erected on a small island in the Basin just off Gay St. in 1764. This is a part of Old Town, the island is gone . . . Across the middle of the original site of Baltimore, ran the Great Road from North to South, on which all the colonies were strung. It was the main street of the village — 'town' — city and remains so today. Crossing the main street was one which was first called Long St., later Market St., and finally Baltimore St. In 1904 the whole middle section was levelled by fire. It was the banking and warehouse district. Over one hundred and forty acres and more than two thousand buildings were destroyed, without damaging a home or taking a life. The fire broke out on a wintry Sunday, Feb 7, 1904 at 11 a.m. when most Baltimoreans were in Church. The fire chief's report, in part said, "It being Sunday and a commercial district, there was no one to look after the numerous incipient fires". It was Jones Falls which provided the firemen with a stand to halt the advance of this great fire.

Near the Falls, the Shot Tower stands guard. The ancient brick tower was the first of its kind in the U.S. It was started in June and completed in November 1828. The cornerstone was laid by Charles Carroll of Carrollton and no external scaffolding was used in building the tower. It took over a million bricks to complete. The battlement top was added much later.

Today, the Inner Harbor has been rejuvenated, in an effort to restore some of the former glory and put back the charm in "Charm City". The new buildings, tall and sleek, will add to the graciousness and elegance, along with the U.S.F. Constellation, and the "Pride of Baltimore" — the new mall, the spacious plaza, with glimpses of the restoration and rebirth of quaint row houses.

The sea has always been the life's blood of Baltimore, carrying to it the spices and tea for McCormick's from the Spice Islands, and banana boats from Puerto Rico and Cuba and the sugar boats for the Sugar Refinery. Exotic cargoes from exotic lands. And the exports from this abundant land, tobacco, corn, wheat, copper, marble (hence the famous white marble steps of Baltimore) famous fish and shell fish, world renowned; all shipped from this hub of commerce, 'the Branch' — the Inner Harbor'.

MEMO

To entertain should be fun.

Nothing is more devastating than to spend the whole day preparing a superb meal for your expected guests and then feel too exhausted to enjoy their company.

As often as possible these recipes have been arranged for the least effort, but resulting in the maximum effect.

The colonial recipes are not only fun to read, but, also to prepare — when you feel experimental!

Kissing don't last,
Cookery do!

George Meredith
(1818—1909)

13

MEASURES WITHOUT MISERY

Converting recipes with total accuracy, these days can often reduce the calmest of us to a trembling mass.

Ingredients vary in bulk, of course, but if you use the chart, adding and subtracting where necessary — your cooking will not suffer. Even more important, you will retain your sanity!

1 teaspoon = 5g. = 5ml.
3 teaspoons = 15g. = 15ml. = U.S. tablespoon
4 teaspoons = 20g. = 20ml. = 1 English tablespoon

Solids

  1 oz. = 1½ tablespoons (English) = U.S. table-
          spoons = 30g.
  2 oz. = 3 tablespoons (English) = 4 U.S. table-
          spoons = ¼ cup = 60g.
  4 oz. = ½ cup = 125g. (well almost!)
  8 oz. = 1 cup = 250g.
16 oz. = 1 lb. = 2 cups = 500g.

Liquids

  1 fl. oz. = 2 U.S. tablespoons = 1½ English
          = 30ml.
  2 fl. oz. = 4 U.S. tablespoons = 3 English
          = ¼ cup = 60ml.
  4 fl. oz. = ¼ U.S.-European pint = ½ cup
          = 125 ml.
  5 fl. oz. = ¼ English pint = 5/8 cup = 150ml.
  8 fl. oz. = ½ U.S.-European pint = 1 cup
          = 250ml.
10 fl. oz. = ½ English pint = 1¼ cups = 300ml.
16 fl. oz = 1 U.S.-European pint = 2 cups
          = 500ml.
20 fl. oz = 1 English pint = 2½ cups = 625ml.
32 fl. oz. = 2 U.S.-European pints = 1 quart
          = 1 litre

Before

The

Main

Course

The early Marylanders
brought their Sherry
with them,
so serve a glass
before dinner —
or after,
if you prefer.

Room temperature

Leonard Calvert. Governor
1635-1647

PATÉ de BURGUNDIE

A touch of FRENCH cuisine is a delicious appetizer, relatively economical and impressive.

> 6 ozs. sausage meat or skinned sausages
> 8 ozs. chicken livers
> 1 egg
> pinch of salt
> Fresh ground black pepper
> 1 tsp Thyme and Basil mixed
> 1 tbs brandy
> 3 tbs muscatel sherry or port
> strips of pork or bacon fat

Remove stringy pieces from livers and puree in blender. Mix puree with sausage, rest of ingredients, except fat strips, put into pint terrine, arrange fat strips on top, stand in pan of boiling water and bake for 45 minutes in a 400 degree oven. The flavours are enhanced and developed by keeping for a couple of days before serving.

Your own homemade corn bread is delicious with this Paté.

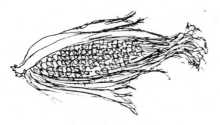

From a Relation of Maryland, published in 1635.

"In the first place I name Corne, as the thing most necessary to sustain man. That which the Natives use in the countrey makes very good bread; and also a meat which they call "Omene" (hominy) and is very savoury and wholesome."

The statue of Major-General Samuel Smith, merchant-soldier

Hero of both wars for American Independence, stands in the Federal Hill Park.

He fought at the battles of:

Long Island
White Plains
Brandywine
Defender of
  Fort Miflin
Valley Forge
Monmouth
Baltimore

SAMUEL SMITH

17

CREAM DIP

The variations of this dip are limitless, try serving it with raw vegetables. Wash and dry mushrooms, cauliflower pieces, cucumber, celery, green pepper and carrot sticks. They can be prepared well ahead, wrapped in plastic and chilled in the refrigerator till needed.

Here is the basic recipe,

Combine
> 8 ozs carton sour cream
> 1 ½ tablespoons mayonnaise
> 1 teaspoon lemon juice
> ½ teaspoon salt
> Freshly ground pepper

Now the variations begin, as the mood takes you,

> Curry powder, paprika and chopped parsley,
> Soy sauce, chopped fresh ginger, water chestnuts and chives.
> Hard-boiled eggs and caviar
> Chopped capsicum, celery and shallots
> Chopped walnuts, ½ clove garlic and chopped cucumber peeled and seeded.

You can substitute horseradish for the mayonnaise. Use cream cheese instead of sour cream, or yoghurt instead of mayonnaise.

The possibilities are as endless as your creativity.

Here is a colonial recipe for **CHEESE STRAWS** from the kitchen of Hampton House.

Take equal parts of flour and snappy American cheese ground in food chopper, a little salt and a little paprika. Mix with ice water like pie crust. Roll out very thin and line your tin. Then cut into lengths and bake 10 or 12 minutes.

A. Brillat Savarin, a famous French gourmet, said, "The discovery of a new dish does more for human happiness than the discovery of a new star".

CRABMEAT STUFFED MUSHROOMS are a delicious appetizer or side dish.

You will need,

    12 large white mushrooms
    7 ozs. crabmeat
    1 teaspoon cornstarch
    2 scallions, finely chopped
    1 teaspoon dry sherry
    ½ teaspoon powdered ginger
    1 egg white
    salt and freshly ground pepper
    2 tablespoons peanut oil
    1 tablespoon soy sauce

Wash and remove stems from mushrooms. Mince crabmeat and place in mixing bowl. Mix ginger with cornstarch, then mix cornstarch with water. Add scallions, sherry, cornstarch mixture and egg with the crabmeat. Mix well, adding salt and pepper to taste. Stuff mushrooms with crabmeat mixture. Place mushrooms in heavy skillet, large enough to hold all 12 mushrooms in one layer. Add ¼ cup water, oil and soy sauce. Bring to boiling and cover. Reduce heat and cook 10 minutes, drain and serve while hot.

TO DRESS A CRAB

"Having taken out the meat, and cleaned it from the skin put it in a stew-pan with half a pint of white wine, a little nutmeg, pepper and salt, over a low fire. Throw in a few crumbs of bread, heat up one yolk of an egg with one spoonful of vinegar, throw it in, then shake the sauce round a minute, and serve it on a plate".

Mrs. Hannah Glasse, "The Art of Cookery Made Plain and Easy". 1812

Warren Ave
Federal Hill, circa 1790

Warren Ave., Federal Hill, adjoins the park. This charming
group overlook the Park and the Harbor.

STEWED OYSTERS IN FRENCH ROLLS

*Take any quantity of oysters and wash them in
their own liquor. Then, straining it, put it in
again with them and add a little salt, ground
pepper, mace and grated nutmeg. Let them stew
a little together and thicken with a great deal of
butter. In the meantime cut the tops off a few
French rolls and take out sufficient crumbs to
admit some of the oysters, which must be filled
in boiling hot and set over a stove, or chafing
dish of hot coals, till they are quite hot through,
filling them up with more liquor, or some hot
gravy as the former soaks in. When they are
sufficiently moistened, serve them up in the
manner of puddings.*

THE HOUSEKEEPERS GUIDE
M. Radcliffe. 1822

An elegant and unique variation of the recipe
calls for champagne in which to simmer the
oysters with seasonings and herbs and a little
arrowroot for thickening. The bread rolls were
heated first and individually wrapped in foil,
filled and served with more champagne . . . . . .
delicious!

SPINACH TART is a favourite of many people. But many people won't prepare it because the pastry case is a bother to make. This is for them.

Boil in their skins 4 medium potatoes
Remove skins, mash well, no lumps.
Add 2 ½ tablespoons of flour,
4 tablespoons soft butter or margarine
salt and pepper to taste
Roll out on lightly floured board to ¼ inch thickness and spread onto greased and floured flan tin, as pastry. Prick base with fork.

Combine

4 oz packed cream cheese
7 ½ oz can of reduced cream

Mix in

¼ cup shredded tasty cheese
2 large beaten eggs
½ teasoon tarragon leaves
1 teaspoon salt
2 cups spinach with 1 sliced onion cooked very slowly in covered saucepan without water until tender, drain spinach well, pressing out excess water, chop again and cool.

Fry

1 cup sliced mushrooms in
1 tablespoon butter, until soft.
Mix mushrooms into cream and egg mixture, add spinach and onion, well drained, and pour into prepared pastry case. Bake in 350 degree oven for approximately 40 minutes. Let stand for 7 minutes before serving, garnish with lemon slices serves 4-6.

Housewives who run up bills become the slaves of tradesmen and can possess no proper independence of principle or self-respect.

H.S.C. COOKERY AND DOMESTIC ECONOMY
FOR YOUNG HOUSEWIVES. 1838

MOUNT CLARE

Mount Clare

New Year's Day collation at Mount Clare

Crab Imperial   *Oyster Loaves*
Boned Turkey Breast
with forcemeat and Oyster Sauce
Fried Chicken   *Maryland Ham*
Fruits in White wine jelly
Beaten biscuits   *Sally Lunn*
Apricot Fool
Apple Float   *Minced Pies*
Pound Cake   *Light Fruit Cake*
Maryland Rocks   *Little Sugar Cakes*
Coconut Jumbles
Peach Cordial   *Syllabub*   *Egg Nog*
Sangaree

Mount Clare, the Mansion house of Margaret and
Charles Carroll, Barrister, once stood on 848
acres looking down to the Patapsco River a mile
away; it is, today, in the heart of Baltimore.

LEEK AND PUMPKIN SOUP

1 lb diced pumpkin
½ lb diced potatoes
1 large onion sliced
2 ozs. butter
4 ozs. green beans
1 cup dried milk powder
2 cups water
salt and pepper (cayenne) to taste
2 leeks sliced
2 cups chicken stock
1 cup cooked rice
¾ cup sour cream
2 tablespoons chopped parsley

Simmer the diced vegetables in half the butter, add sliced beans, milk powder and water and simmer ½ hour, stir often. Then purée or use blender, season to taste. Sauté leeks in remaining butter add to soup, with chicken stock, simmer a few minutes before mixing in cream and rice. Then reheat without boiling and serve with chopped parsley as garnish. Serves 4-6.

'The first drugstore in Baltimore was established in 1746 by Dr. William Lyon at the Corner of Market (now Baltimore) Street and Calvert Street.'

John R. Quinlan. "Medical Annals of Baltimore"
Baltimore 1884

VICHYSSOISE is certainly one of the most popular cold soups and despite its French name is really an American invention.

3 cups cooked potatoes, peeled and sliced
3 cups cooked leeks, white end, sliced
6 cups chicken stock (no seasoning)
Blend in electric blender till smooth.
Chill in refrigerator, then add
1 cup fresh cream, season to taste (more salt than with a hot soup)
Refrigerate overnight and top with chopped chives when served.

1 Montgomery St. Sth. Baltimore

1 Montgomery Street, Sth. Baltimore

One of the streets adjacent to Federal Hill, with many picturesque houses restored to former glory.

Baltimore's first official postmaster was a woman, Mary K. Goddard, sister of William Goddard. Appointed in 1775 she served until 16th Feb 1790. On December 1793, she was re-appointed to the position by direction of George Washington, and held the position until 1800.

CREAM OF MUSHROOM SOUP always creates enthusiasm. For the small amount of time or effort it takes, the result is always gratifying.

Melt
> 1 oz. of butter or margarine
> Add ½ lb. to 1½ lb. mushroom (depending on your budget, but the more the better) broken into bite sized pieces.
> 1 white onion peeled and sliced very thin and sauted, stirring for a couple of minutes

Add
> 2 cups chicken stock and simmer gently, covered, for 10 minutes

Combine
> 1 tablespoon cornstarch with
> ½ cup of milk and add to the mushrooms, together with
> 2 cups chicken stock
> Heat, stirring until thickened.
> Blend in one can undiluted cream of chicken soup and 1 can undiluted cream of mushroom soup. Season to taste.
> Reheat, when ready to serve, stir in 4 ozs. sour cream and sprinkle top literally with chopped chives.

SUMMER SOUP MARINARA is really delectable

Mix together in a soup tureen or serving bowl
> 1 large chicken stock cube dissolved in
> 1 cup boiling water, cooled. Then mix in
> 8 oz. carton of plain yoghurt
> 8 oz. container cream
> 30 fl. oz. can tomato juice
> 1 large cucumber, peeled seeded and diced
> ½ lb. bresh crabmeat or shrimp
> Add a little freshly ground black pepper and dash of garlic salt, but taste first, before you add salt, sometimes the chicken cube makes it salty enough.

"Females should be early taught to prefer the society of their homes, to engage themselves in domestic duties, and to avoid every species of idle vanity, to which thousands of them owe their ruin."

The Housekeepers Guide
M. Radcliffe, 1822

Federal Hill Park looking towards
Warren Avenue

During the Civil War the Union troops used Federal Hill as fortification. To ensure that the city remained in Union hands the cannon were set, aimed directly towards the city, just as a friendly reminder!

"In the Spring are several sorts of Herbs, a corn-sallet, violets sorrell, pursalaine — all of which are very good and wholesome and by the English used for sallets and broth"

Leonard Calvert to his brother Lord Baltimore in England

Indian tribes gave early settlers a great deal of trouble, so much so, that they were declared public enemies by Governor Calvert. A treaty was finally made with them in 1652.

The Sasquehannocks tribe were very powerful between 1606-1662 at which time they held several fortified towns along the river banks. A 10-12 ft. high palisade enclosed numerous cabins (wigwoms) a water supply and fire place. The outside fields of corn and tobacco were held in common for the village.

Some tribes lived in harmony with the new settlers and showed them the many uses of corn and wild fruits and fowl. They exchanged ideas on crop cultivation and there passed a time of peace and tranquility with mutual help.

However Col. Claiborne of Kent Island soon began a campaign to undermine the settlers peaceful intent and he and his cohorts went amongst the Indians spreading fear and hatred by saying the settlers were really going to take all the land and kill all the Indians. On occasions some of Claiborne's men would swoop on Indian villages and burn and pillage to prove his point.

LITTLE INDIAN CAKES

Put a spoonful of lard in a quart of meal, and two teaspoonsful of salt, pour boiling water on half the meal, stir it; then add as much cold water as will enable you to make it out in cakes of a convenient size; bake on the bake-iron (griddle) over the fire.

Elizabeth Rea
Baltimore 1853

28

The

Main

Course

SOFT SHELL CRAB

A recipe from Margaret Tilghman Carroll's letterbook of receipts. Buy fresh from the fishmonger and be sure he has removed the "sandbag", "deadmen", and "apron". Rinse, pat dry, and roll crabs lightly in flour, salt and pepper. Melt some lard and butter, approximately half and half, in an iron skillet about ¼ inch deep. Fry crabs until golden brown, about 5 minutes on each side. Allow 2 per person and eat everything, claws and all! This delicacy is beautiful to behold, simple to prepare, and delicious to taste. It is so sweet and succulent it needs no sauce.

CRAB CAKES *are another Maryland delight. This Hampton House recipe is simple and delicious.*

Take 1 lb. of crab meat for each four crab cakes. Put crab meat into a mixing bowl, add 1½ teaspoons salt, 1 teaspoon white pepper, 1 teaspoon English dry mustard and 2 teaspoons Worcestershire sauce, 1 egg yolk and 1 soup spoon cream sauce or mayonnaise, 1 teaspoon chopped parsley. Mix well, making four crab cakes, press hard together, dip into flour, then into beaten eggs, then into breadcrumbs. Fry them in hot grease.

Mt Clare Station 1830, included in B & O Museum. The 1844 Round house with original tracks and wooden turntable are masterfully preserved and on display, with an extensive collection of railroad artifacts.

FRIED OYSTERS

25 oysters drained
¼ teaspoon pepper
3 eggs, beaten
1/8 teaspoon cayenne
1 cup bread crumbs or
cracker crumbs, finely pounded
lard or other fat for deep frying
1 teaspoon salt

Dip oysters in beaten eggs. Remove them and roll in the bread crumbs, or cracker meal, which have been highly seasoned with salt, pepper and cayenne. Pat meal or crumbs onto oysters with your hands to coat well. Fry oysters in hot fat in a deep skillet until brown. Serve 4 to each person as an appetizer or 8 for a main dish. Serve garnished with parsley and lemons.

FLOUNDER FILETS IN WINE

6 flounder fillets
4 scallions chopped
½ cup dry white wine or sherry
1½ tbsp. fresh parsley, chopped
½ tsp. powdered sage
2 bay leaves, finely crushed
salt and white pepper
sweet butter
2 tsp. cornstarch
3 tbsp. light cream

Heat oven to 350 degrees F. Lay fillets in baking dish, cover with scallions, wine, parsley, sage, bay leaves, salt and pepper to taste. Dot with butter. Cover fish with foil and bake 25 minutes. Remove fillets carefully with broad lift or spatula to warm serving dish. Melt butter in saucepan, blend in cornstarch and cream over low heat. Add juices from baking dish, stirring continually until sauce is smooth. Cook slowly for 3 minutes pour over fish and serve, immediately.

"The first water company to be chartered in the United States was the Baltimore Water Company, which was founded in 1792".

31

CHICKEN MARYLAND has travelled the world, it appears on menus in almost every country. However, it is not always prepared correctly. Here is the way Margaret Carroll prepared it for her family and guests.

> 1 cup flour approximately
> ¼ cup fresh bacon fat
> salt and pepper to taste
> 1½ cups lard
> 3 to 3½ lbs. frying chicken, cut in pieces

Put flour seasoned with salt and pepper into a paper bag. Add chicken pieces and shake to coat thoroughly. Heat fat and lard in a large iron skillet, the fat should be deep enough to cover at least half the chicken. Put chicken in the hot fat and turn when it is a deep brown, about 10 to 15 minutes. Cover the pan for part of the remaining cooking time. When done, drain the chicken on absorbent paper. Do not refrigerate. If you wish, a delicious cream gravy can be made by skimming off the excess fat from the pan drippings and adding milk and cooked chopped giblets. Cook until thickened, stirring constantly.

To accompany Chicken Maryland, there should be Broiled Bacon Strips and

CORN FRITTERS

Drain and chop 1 cup fresh or canned whole kernal corn. Add 1 beaten egg yolk. Stir in ½ cup sifted flour with ½ teaspoon baking powder, ¼ teaspoon salt and pinch of pepper. Add ¼ cup milk, fold in stiffly beaten egg white. Drop by tablespoons into deep or shallow fat, heated to 375 degrees F. Cook for 5 minutes until golden brown. Drain on absorbent paper. These are just as delicious for breakfast with syrup, or as an accent to ham or pork sausages.

"Female servants should be circumspect in their conduct towards the male servants; too much freedom may occasion improper liberties, and too much reserve may produce disgust and hatred . . ."

MODERN DOMESTIC COOKERY
ELIZABETH HAMMOND, 1825

32

Father Andrew White S.J. in his account of the voyage to Maryland, mentions in glowing terms of the fruit he tasted during the stopover in "the Charybbian Ilands, which run up like a bow in the Bay of Mexico . . . . ." ". . . . but the rarest of all other that I thinke is in the world — is the Charybbian Pinaple, of the colour of gould, mixed with an orient greene, ... of delitious taste not having one membranula or kernell, but all, from highest part to lowest, cleane through equally dainty to taste. It beares in the toppe Crowne of its owne leaves . . . for sure it is the queene of all meat fruits without exception."
Partridge and game hens were readily available in the early days of Maryland. Fortunately for us, both Pineapple and Game hens are even more accessible, in the local supermarket. Here is a recipe which would gladden the heart of any Marylander in any year, which combines

GAME HENS AND PINEAPPLE

    1 x 20 oz. can of crushed pineapple
    2 x game hens
    salt and pepper'

Drain pineapple, keep 1 cup of syrup.
Sprinkle hens with salt and pepper.
Stuff hens with pineapple stuffing.

    1 cup diced celery
    1 cup diced onion
    2 tablespoons butter
    1 cup crushed pineapple
    1 cup cooked brown rice
    ¼ cup raisins
    ½ teaspoon thyme leaves
    1/8 teaspoon sage rubbed and crumbled
    ½ teaspoon salt

Saute celery and green onion in butter till celery is tender. Remove from heat and stir in pineapple, rice, raisins, thyme, sage and salt.

Truss hens, place any leftover stuffing in foil and set beside hens on roasting rack. Bake in 400 degree oven for 20 minutes. Reduce heat to 350 degrees and roast for 30 minutes longer, brushing generously every 15 minutes with currant glaze:

> 1 cup pineapple syrup, any leftover crushed pineapple, ½ cup currant jam, 2 tablespoons dry sherry, 2 tablespoons cornstarch, 1/8 tablespoon onion powder.

Combine pineapple, syrup and jam until blended. Cook over low heat until jam is melted. Combine sherry, cornstarch and onion powder, add to pineapple mixture, cook until mixture is clear and thickened.

This recipe serves two, allowing 1 bird each; for smaller appetites, ½ a bird may be sufficient when accompanied by side dishes. Small, whole potatoes with parsley butter and fresh green peas.

While geese are not running the streets any more, sometimes a lucky hunter brings one home. So, here is a recipe which makes use of another modern kitchen helper, the crock-pot.

CROCKED GOOSE

> 1 wild goose, skinned and boned
> 4 onions quartered
> 4 ribs of celery, diced
> 1 small can whole tomatoes cut in pieces
> 1 cup dry red wine
> 1 cup strong beef stock
> ½ tsp. onion salt, pinch garlic salt, fresh ground pepper, 1 tsp Worcestershire sauce

Cut goose flesh in strips. Combine with remaining ingredients in a slow cooker, (crock-pot). Cover, cook on high setting for approximately 5 hours. Serve in a chafing dish for buffet. Serve with steamed rice, broccoli or brussel sprouts as vegetable.

34

No book of recipes for the Inner Harbor area would be complete without a reminder of the gastronomic delights prepared by the German and Irish Settlers.

First SAUERBRATEN or as we call it

SOUR BEEF AND DUMPLINGS

> 5 lbs. beef cut into cubes
> 4 large onions, diced
> 1 cup vinegar and 1 cup water
> Sugar to taste, salt to taste
> Pepper to taste, 15 ginger snaps
> Pickling spices
> 5 lbs. potatoes, 2 slices of bread cubed
> Flour and oil

Make spice bag by tying spices in cheese cloth bag. Put beef cubes, 3 onions, vinegar, water, salt, pepper and sugar in a saucepan. Bring this to boil, simmer till meat is tender. Put some of broth over ginger snaps to make a paste. Add this paste mixture to the meat pot until mixture is thickened.

DUMPLINGS Peel potatoes, cook half of this amount and mash, then grate the other half. Put the raw potatoes into a cloth bag and squeeze out excess water. Add to mashed potatoes. Saute bread cubes along with remaining onion (diced), until onion is soft and bread is browned. Cool both mixtures, then add both bread and onion to potatoes. Form into small balls, adding just enough flour to make the ball hold. Drop these into boiling salted water and cook until they float. Put on a dish and serve with sour beef mixture. Serves 8 − 10.

Letterbooks of Dr. Charles Carroll, Ms/203, Maryland Historical Society.

".... we are in need of a sober, orderly woman of good character that understands Cooking, Pickling, Preserving and other Requisites for a Housekeeper. If elderley we shall Like her the Better. She must not be of the flirting kind or one that will give herself airs. If above the ordinary rank of servants, my wife will Like her Better as she will meet with all kind treatment."

STEAK DIANE FLAMBÉ is a glamorous dish for when you want to impress your guests.

> 8 x 4 oz. tenderloin fillets
> salt and pepper
> 6 tablespoons clarified butter
> 8 ozs. sliced mushrooms
> ¼ cup shallots
> 1 tablespoon chopped parsley
> 1 teaspoon chopped chives
> ¼ cup French brandy
> 2 tablespoons Madeira wine
> 2 tablespoons steak sauce
> ½ tablespoon Worcestershire Sauce

Season meat with salt and pepper. Melt butter in skillet over medium heat. Add mushrooms, cook for 2 minutes, add shallots, parsley, chives and cook for 2 minutes more. Remove vegetables, retain butter in pan, increase heat and cook 4 fillets at a time, 2 to 3 minutes per side for rare or medium rare.

Return vegetables and meat to pan; add Cognac. Flame. When flame is out add beef broth, wine steak sauce and Worcestershire Sauce. Cook for 1 minute, season to taste, serve with wild rice. Serves 4 persons.

"Change of food is to the stomach what change of air is to the general health . . . "
> *THE MODERN HOUSEWIFE*
> *ALEXIS SOYER*

The earliest known black emigrants to Maryland came over on the "Ark and the Dove" in 1694. They were Mathias Stone and John Price. There may have been a third, a man named Mimus, but no clear information is available.

Benjamin Anneker (1731–1803) was the first black scientist in America. He taught himself, and became a very skilful astronomer. He was a friend of Major Andrew Ellicott, became his special assistant in the survey of the District of Columbia. Upon his return to Maryland, he produced almanacs for 1792 through 1797. A remarkable man!

A ROSTE

A recipe from the early 16th century
Roast beef with crisps.

4—5 tbspns oil for searing meat
5 pound boned rib roast rolled and tied
½ cup flour
1 tspn cinnamon
1 tspn dried sweet basil
½ tspn dried rosemary
¼ tspn thyme
1 cup dates, pitted and halved
1 cup dried figs, cut in strips
½ cup dried apple rings, halved
2 tbspns honey
1½ cups beef stock

Batter
1 cup flour, 1 egg, 2/3 cup milk,
¼ tspn salt, ½ level tspn baking powder
¼ cup finely chopped parsley

Mode
Preheat oven to 350°F
Melt butter in a Dutch oven or any heavy
metal pot with tight fitting lid. Dredge the
meat with the mixture of flour, cinnamon,
and salt, searing thoroughly in heated oil,
browning all over. Mix thyme, basil and rosemary.
Combine spices with dates, figs and apples.
Place spiced fruits around meat in Dutch
oven. Drizzle honey on fruits. Carefully
pour beef stock around edges of pot to avoid
washing herbs etc. off fruits. Tightly cover.
Bake until tender, approximately three hours.
Remove from oven and leave to cool for 30
minutes. Turn up oven heat to 450°F.
Beat together all batter ingredients except
parsley, to make a very thick batter. Use
more flour if necessary. Stir in chopped
parsley. Turn out batter over meat so that
it trickles into gravy. Put meat back in the
oven without lid on pot and the batter blanket
should brown nicely in about 10 minutes.
Slice the roast and serve with the crisps that
have cooked in the juices on the bottom of
the pot, along with the gravy and fruit.
This is slightly reminiscent of Yorkshire
Pudding or Beef Wellington.

ORANGE GLAZED PORK CHOPS

Trim fat from 4 good sized pork chops. Heat fat in frying pan and when you have about 1 tablespoon of melted fat, remove trimmings. Brown chops on both sides in hot fat, season with salt and pepper. Drain off excess fat. Combine 1 tablespoon brown sugar, 2 tablespoons orange marmalade, ½ cup orange juice and 1 tablespoon vinegar and pour over chops. Simmer until chops are done. Remove chops to warm platter, bring sauce to boiling and spoon over chops. Serves 4.

The first demonstration of gas lighting of a building in North America was given by Benjamin Henfrey, an Englishman resident in Baltimore, in 1802. He installed a gas-lighting system of his own devising in the ballroom of a Mr. Robardett on Second Street (now Water Street). Alas! He was ahead of his time and no one in the city was convinced of the potential of the new lighting system.

"I didn't know that"
Maryland Historical Society

VCP

Thames Street has not lost its waterfront charm, it still looks like a street in Marseilles.

Fell's Point has so many charming restaurants of all nations, it is difficult to make a choice; Little Italy has always been a favourite part of the Point and in honor of the many great cooks there, here is a simple and enjoyable culinary delight, **FETTUCINE**

> 12 ozs. Fettucine noodles
> ½ cup heavy cream
> 6 tbsp. unsalted butter (softened)
> 3 ozs. grated Parmesan cheese
> 6 ozs. frozen peas
> ½ lb. prosciutto, sliced thinly and cut in thin strips
> Black pepper to taste

Cook Fettucine noodles, heat cream. Drain noodles, add softened butter and Parmesan cheese, toss lightly and quickly. Add heated cream, peas and prosciutto and pepper to taste. Toss again lightly and serve quickly.

Shot Tower and (1828)
9 North Front Street (1794)

THE SHOT TOWER is the last remaining one in the United States. Molten lead used to be poured down inside from the top and the drops of lead cooled as they fell, making the shot. Better ways of making shot were soon developed, but the Shot Tower remains as a beloved historic landmark.

9 North Front Street is in the Shot Tower Park.

It has had a chequered career. Its claim to fame is that
the second Mayor of Baltimore, Thorowgood Smith
lived there, and later the family of Edgar Allen Poe. The
house was built in 1794, originally part of a row of
houses since demolished. After much work and fund
raising, the Women's Civic League restored it in 1976,
as a bi-centennial project. It is leased to them as their
headquarters. It is well worth a visit, as it is close to the
Carroll Mansion, and the Flag House.

Now for some side dishes to accompany your favourite meat or fish or fowl.

RATATOUILLE is popular with most good cooks, and guests.

> 1 medium eggplant, peeled and cut in chunks of 1 inch
> 4 medium zucchini thinly sliced
> 2 medium green peppers cut in thin strips
> 2 medium tomatoes cut in thin wedges
> 1 cup chopped onion
> 1 cup bottled sweet, spicy french dressing
> 1 tbsp. chopped fresh basil or 1 tsp. dried

Combine all ingredients in large saucepan. Cover and simmer for 30 to 40 minutes, stirring occasionally until vegetables are just tender. Makes about 6 cups.

Carroll Mansion (1822)
E. Lombard St.

East Lombard Street is where Charles Carroll of Carrollton built the great Town House for his daughter, Mrs. Harper. It was here that the signer of the Declaration of Independence finally closed his eyes in eternal sleep.

42

Another side dish from the "Art of Cooking Made Plain and Easy" by Mrs. Glasse printed by Colton and Stewart in 1812.

RED CABBAGE *dressed after the Dutch Way, good for a cold on the Breast.*

Take the cabbage, cut it small and boil it soft, then drain it and put it in a saucepan, with a sufficient quantity of oil and butter, a little water and vinegar and an onion cut small; season it with pepper and salt, and let it simmer on a slow fire, till all the liquor is wasted."

I am not sure if this was a remedy to be taken by mouth or applied to the affected part!

There is no doubt how we should deal with

STUFFED ONIONS

    6 large onions
    1 lb. bulk pork sausage
    1 tbsp. Worcestershire sauce
    1 cup tomato sauce
    1 tsp. tarragon
    ½ tsp. basil
    ½ tsp. garlic powder
    ½ tsp. salt
    ¼ tsp. pepper

Peel onions and cook in boiling salted water for 20 to 30 minutes. Cool and cut a slice off the top. Scoop out insides, chop and set aside. Mix sausage and Worcestershire sauce, brown meat mixture until it is no longer pink. Drain and cool. Stuff onions with meat mixture, combine chopped onions and tomato sauce, pour over onions. Bake at 350 degrees for 30 minutes.

The Baltimore Department of Health, in continuous operation since the Committee of Health was set up late in 1793, is the oldest permanent municipal body in America (and possibly the world) devoted to public health.

Huntington Williams,
"Baltimore's Health Service150 years old",
Baltimore Health News, Dec. 1943

Two quick ways to prepare vegetables with a different twist.

First CELERY AND WALNUTS

Cut celery into small pieces and chop some walnuts — toss into hot butter for several minutes and serve with a grill.

Second BRUSSELS SPROUTS

Simmer 1 lb. Brussels Sprouts for about 15 minutes, drain well. Place in serving dish or bowl and cover with the following sauce; melt ½ cup butter and as it bubbles blend in 2 tsps. mustard, 1 tsp. Worcestershire sauce, 1/2 tsp. salt and a dash of cayenne pepper.

"To make a Ruta Baga Pudding:

1 ½ pints of pulped Ruta Baga, 2 spoonsful of wheat flour, 4 eggs, 1 ½ pints of milk, and 1 tbsp. butter. The pan greased and floured and baked with a quick fire."

American Farmer — November, 1819

Now in honour of the Irish, a recipe for

CREAMED CABBAGE

> 1 x 2 lb. (approx.) cabbage
> 4 tablespoons flour
> salt and pepper
> 2 tablespoons butter
> ½ teaspoon nutmeg (ground)

Cut cabbage into quarters, remove centre stalk. Soak cabbage in boiling water for 5 minutes, remove from boiling water, drain well. With a sharp knife, cut into narrow wedges. Melt butter in saucepan, put cabbage into melted butter and stir well. Sprinkle flour, nutmeg, salt and pepper over cabbage, mix it through lightly. Return saucepan to *low* heat and add milk stirring gently, so that it does not burn. Cook *very* slowly for 10 − 15 minutes.

Serve with Corned Beef, carrots, onions and potatoes.

The Bank of Baltimore was chartered on Christmas Eve in 1795, 373 days before the City of Baltimore received its charter. The Union Trust company, the direct descendent of the Bank of Baltimore, is now the oldest bank in the state. Its location, St. Paul and Baltimore Streets, is the one originally used in 1795!

"I didn't know that!"
Maryland Historical Society

"Pride of Baltimore"

After

The

Main

Course

"The climate is serene and mild . . . . there are fruitful vines, from which wine can be made and a grape as large as cherries. There are cherries as big as damsons and goose berries just like ours. There are three kinds of plums. Mulberries, chestnuts and walnuts are so plentiful that they are used in various ways for food. Strawberries and raspberries are also to be found for food . . ."

Fr. Andrew White, S.J., his account of the colony 'Narratives of Early Maryland'

PLUMS IN BRANDY

Select those plums that are free from blemish, make a syrup of ½ pound of sugar to 1 pound of fruit. Boil the syrup and skim it. Only let the plums stay in the syrup for 5 minutes. When cool, put them in jars and pour upon them equal quantities of syrup and French brandy. The large amber coloured plums and blue plums are the best.

recipe from
"The Queen of the Kitchen"
by Mrs. Tyson

FROZEN PEACHES

"2 quarts of peach juice (rub the peaches through a collander) 1 pint water, 2 lbs. sugar. When frozen it is very nice."

Coale Collection, Ms. 248
Maryland Historical Society

Dinner for Governor Eden
Before His Departure for England

Dressed Crab

Stuffed Rockfish   *Fried Oyster*

Broiled Game Birds

Maryland Ham   *Chicken & Oyster Pie*

Moulded Spiced Plum Jelly

Carrot Pudding   *Broccoli*

Spoon Bread   *Apricot Nutbread*

Brandied Nectarines   *Pineapple Chutney*

Orange Pudding   *Applesauce Fruit Cake*

Macaroons   *Lemon Cheesecakes*

Punch   *Madiera*   *Port*

Almonds   *Raisins*

Fresh Fruit

Charles Carroll, the Barrister, was chairman of the committee that received Governor Eden in his office in 1776. The night before Maryland's last colonial Governor sailed for England, Mr. Carroll entertained him at dinner. This was the epitome of gracious manners and civility; Marylanders did not hate the Governor himself, they just abhorred his politics. It was probably an affair for gentlemen only, in Annapolis, but Mrs. Carroll would have planned the menu to suit their hearty appetites.

APRICOT FOOL

3 cups mashed apricots, or
2 x 29 oz. cans drained and pureed
2 cups heavy cream, whipped
1 tablespoon sugar
¼ cup orange brandy
Rind of one lemon, grated

Drain apricots, mash to fill 3 cups, then puree in a blender. Stir in liquor, whipped cream sweetened with sugar, and lemon rind. Pour into dessert dishes. Top with preserved ginger or large flakes of sweet chocolate. Serves 8.

A recipe from Margaret Tilghman Carroll
Mount Clare, 1767

Here is a recipe using ice cream which is a breeze to make, and refreshing to eat.

ORANGE BLISS

Allow 1 pint ice cream to thaw slightly, then beat in a bowl until smooth, but still thick and creamy — add ¼ tin frozen orange juice concentrated (thawed) and 2 tablespoons Grand Marnier Liqueur — return to freezer for several hours. Yummy!

"Although Ice Cream had been made in Baltimore and some other parts of the country, it was only on a very small scale. In 1851, Jacob Fussell a milk dealer, started the manufacture of ice cream, as a wholesale production, to use his surplus cream. This was the first wholesale ice cream manufacture and was so well liked at 25 cents a quart, Fussell expanded his business, establishing production plants in Washington and New York City."

"I didn't know that!"
Maryland Historical Society 1973

STRAWBERRIES served with ice cream are not only an instant dessert, they are always an instant success. You can vary your menu by trying a FRUIT BRULEE, cover a layer of fruit with sour cream, then pack brown sugar in a layer, completely covering cream. Place under broiler till sugar caramellises. Serve hot or cold. This can be prepared in individual ovenproof dishes or a larger 1½ to 2 inch deep casserole. Use any fruits in season, seedless grapes, peeled peaches, halved apricots or pears.

"... from the Charybbian Iland ... there is another speciall fruit called a plantaine, singular for pleasant and delightful taste ... They are of curious taste like marmalade and much of that temper, very delightful, fit to preserve, bake or eat raw."

Fr. Andrew White, "Narratives of Maryland"

BUTTERED RUM BANANA CREPES

    6 sweet crepes
    3 bananas
    6 scoops vanilla ice cream

Stir 1 tbsp. cornstarch into ¾ cup of milk in saucepan. Add 1 cup firmly packed brown sugar and ¼ cup light corn syrup, stir continually over medium heat till thickened. Remove from heat, stir in 2 tbsps. butter and 2 tbsps. rum, put aside. On one side of each crepe spread a scoop of softened ice cream. Peel and slice bananas in half lengthwise. Put half a banana on each crepe. Pour warm sauce over filled crepe, top with whipped cream. Serve immediately.

Apples are gold in the morning, silver at noon, and lead at night.
                                                                        AN OLD SAYING

A VERY SIMPLE APPLE CHARLOTTE

Ingredients . . . 9 slices of bread and butter, about 6 good sized apples, 1 tbsp. of minced lemon peel, 2 tbsps. of juice, moist sugar to taste.

MODE . . . Butter a pie dish; place a layer of bread and butter, without the crust, at the bottom; then a layer of apples, pared, cored and cut into thin slices, sprinkle over these a portion of the lemon peel and juice, and sweeten with moist sugar, place another layer of bread and butter and then one of apples proceeding in this manner until the dish is full then cover it with the peel of the apples, to preserve the top from browning or burning, bake in a brisk oven for more than ¾ hour; turn the charlotte on a dish, sprinkle sifted sugar over and serve.

Average cost 1 shilling

Sufficient for 5 or 6 persons

MRS BEETON'S EVERY DAY COOKERY
PUBLISHED AFTER DEATH IN 1865
AGED 29 YEARS

"**Tea Cake** (A Cromwell Family Recipe)

Six large cups flour, 2 tablespoons butter, 2 tablespoons sugar, 4 teaspoonsful baking powder, 2 pints sweet milk and a little salt."

I found no cooking directions, but a hot oven and a greased baking sheet, as for biscuits, would be appropriate. Served hot or cold and spread with butter.

MARRONS SOUFFLE sounds much more glamorous than CHESTNUT CREAM. It has never failed to delight my guests, both here and overseas. It is so easy to make and with all the chestnuts which are available, preparing your own puree is no problem, but for those of us who take the easy way . . . Whip the contents of 1 x 16 oz. can chestnut puree with confectioners sugar to make it sweet but not sickly. Add 1 teaspoon rum essence, and when the mixture is light and creamy, beat in ¼ pint whipping cream and a pinch of salt. Place in souffle dish or individual dishes. Chill, serve with sweetened whipped cream.

"LIGHT HORSE HARRY" LEE'S brilliant army record includes the following recipe for **LEMON SHERBET**

One gallon water, 5 pounds white sugar, juice 16 lemons, ½ box best gelatine. Boil water and sugar together with the rind of one lemon for 15 minutes. Dissolve gelatine in a little cold water and after it is softened put over it the sugar and water syrup until gelatine is entirely dissolved. Then add lemon juice with seeds removed. Do not add lemon juice until the syrup is almost cold. Strain through the cheesecloth and freeze.

From my earliest days in Baltimore, I was delighted with the **LADY BALTIMORE CAKE** and **THE LORD BALTIMORE CAKE**. So, when doing research for this little book, I felt it could not be complete without a recipe for both. However, there are no old colonial recipes for them. They are a relatively modern innovation and didn't even originate in Baltimore! Virginia Roeder, Sun papers, in 1966, discovered that the cake had its origin in Charleston and was created by Mrs. Alicia Rhett Mayberry, one of that city's former belles. At the turn of the century it was quite popular, and was served at a tea room called The Lady Baltimore Tea Room. Owen Wister, who wrote "The Virginian", chose Charleston for the setting of his novel "Lady Baltimore". Since the title of the book came from the cake created by Mrs. Mayberry, and the book was obviously popular, Lady Baltimore Cake soon became *the* cake in the United States. The variations are endless, but the cake layers always seem to be similar, WHITE CAKE for **LADY BALTIMORE** and YELLOW layers, square 7 or 8 inch, for **LORD BALTIMORE**.

Use WHITE CAKE MIXES to make two 11 inch layers. After baking, make a thick syrup of 1 cup sugar and ½ cup water. Flavor with almond and vanilla. Spread this over the layers as soon as you remove them from the pans.

FROSTING AND FILLING

> 3 cups sugar
> 1 teaspoon vanilla
> 1 cup water
> ½ cup chopped figs
> ¼ teaspoon cream of tartar
> 1 cup chopped raisins
> 3 egg whites, stiffly beaten
> 1 cup chopped pecans
> (soak raisins and figs in sherry or
> brandy overnight if desired)

Boil sugar, water and cream of tartar together till it forms a soft ball in cold water. Pour hot syrup over beaten egg whites, beating constantly until of spreading consistency. Add vanilla. Divide mixture in half. Add fruit and nuts to one portion and spread between layers of cake. Frost top and sides with remaining portion.

LORD BALTIMORE CAKE

Using yellow cake mixes make 3 square 7 inch layers.

FILLING AND FROSTING

    3 cups sugar
    1 cup water
    ¼ teaspoon cream of tartar
    3 egg whites, stiffly beaten
    ½ cup rolled dry macaroons or
    ½ cup toasted coconut
    ½ cup toasted, chopped blanched almonds
    12 candied cherries
    2 teaspoons lemon juice
    3 teaspoons sherry or brandy

Boil sugar and water and cream of tartar together until a small amount forms a soft ball in cold water. Pour hot syrup gradually over beaten egg whites, beating constantly until of spreading consistency. Divide mixture in half. Add remaining ingredients to one portion and spread between layers of cake. Frost top and sides with remaining portion. The last Lord Baltimore Cake I made, I decorated the top with a lattice design which I piped on and then added halves of maraschino cherries on the corners. It was elaborate but very attractive for a special occasion!

Thames St.
Fells Pt.

FELL'S POINT, where the cobblestones are really cobblestones brought from distant sea beaches as ballast in the holds of clipper ships; as were the bricks used for paving and laid in the herring-bone or chevron pattern you can see down on the Fort McHenry walks. Fell's Point is the home of many of the European settlers. Italian, Polish, Jewish, Greek, Slovakian and so on. You will find quaint little restaurants or bistros serving an exciting variety of foods. The

atmosphere is very much like the Left Bank in
Paris — or the Barbary Coast in San Francisco,
lively, colorful and enjoyable. The houses and
shops are being restored and rejuvenated like the
other parts of old Baltimore. Behind the Point,
empties the Harford Run which used to be part
of the canal system; but that's another story!
There are lots of little streets which keep in
touch with the waterfront, lined with leafy trees
to shade the doorways, and windows filled with
growing plants.

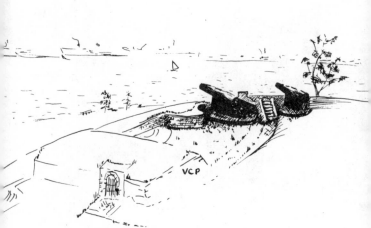

VCP

"Then let the old fort stand intact, the
proudest of our shrines,
Her deathless glory ever linked with Key's
immortal lines;
... And generations yet unborn shall to her
slopes repair,
And gazing on her streaming flag, rejoice
to see it there."

from the poem "Ft. McHenry"
by Charles T. Duvall,
The Maryland Scene, 1943
Remington Putnum Book Co.

The Star Fort was begun in 1794 and later
named for Washington's Secretary of War in
1795. The fort is built in the shape of a star with
high stone walls, earth covered and grown over
with grass. The gallant defense of Baltimore in
1814 inspired the writing of the anthem "The
Star Spangled Banner". The fort today is a
gracious step back into history. The restoration
and maintenance is a great credit to those
dedicated people who have saved a piece of
history for us to enjoy.

The Walkway outside the Officer's Quarters, Ft. McHenry

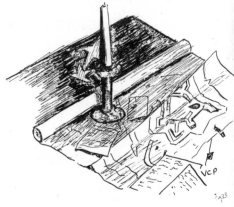

Fort McHenry, commanded by Col. George Armistead during the bombardment by the British Fleet Sept. 13—14, 1814, during the War of 1812. This was a war of commercial freedom, due to the overbearing conduct of England in taking men by force into the British Navy, from American trading ships, and generally disrupting trade.

Beverages

During the repast, or after the last plates have been cleared away and your guests still sit around the dinner table; it is time to enjoy the conversation . . .

IRISH COFFEE is for the host or hostess who likes a touch of the dramatic when they entertain.

In each pre-warmed Irish Whiskey glass — or cup pour

>   1 tablespoon Irish Whiskey and ignite it.

Then add immediately

>   ½ cup hot strong coffee
>   1 teaspoon raw sugar

Stir until sugar is dissolved.

Float lightly whipped cream on top.

Do not stir . . . the coffee should be sipped through the cream.

Coffee is not the only way to conclude a delicious dinner, try this **RUSSIAN TEA**

>   5 oranges
>   1 lemon
>   1½ cups sugar
>   rind of two oranges

Boil all together for ten minutes . . . gently . . . and strain. Mix with 8 cups of strong tea. Drop in 6 cloves. Serves about 20. This should be tasted before serving, adding more of this or that, to suit the individual.

Recipe from Hampton House

*Since we have reached the Ft. McHenry drawings
it seems appropriate to introduce the*

ARTILLERYMAN'S PUNCH

    18 ozs. Bourbon
    6 ozs. light rum
    3 ozs. dark Jamaica rum
    3 ozs. apricot brandy
    6 ozs. lemon juice
    18 ozs. very strong black tea
    2 lemons sliced

Place all ingredients in punch bowl over large
block of ice. Let mixture stand for at least
30 minutes. (Or place in pitcher). Serve in
pre-chilled glasses. Makes 12, 6 oz. serves.

How anyone could shoot straight after a couple
of these, is hard to imagine!

A **TOAST**, to go with the punch . . .

*"Here's to our wives, who fill our lives
with little bees and honey;
They break life's shocks, they mend our socks,
But don't they spend our money!"*

COLONIAL RECIPES
BOMBERGER

Sketch of **Col. George Armistead,**

Commander of Ft. McHenry
during the bombardment,
1814.

ARMISTEAD

61

When Martha Washington passed through Baltimore on her way to New York for the first inauguration, she stopped at Mount Clare. Mrs. Carroll entertained the new First Lady's entourage with refreshments. "We found a large bowl of salubrious punch, with fruits etc. which had been plucked from trees in a green house, lying on the tables in great abundance; these, after riding 25 or 30 miles without eating or drinking, was no unwelcome luxury; however, Mrs. C could not complain that we had not done her punch honor, for in the course of one quarter of an hour (the time we tarried) this bowl, which held upwards of two gallons was entirely consumed to the no little satisfaction of us all." ... from Robert Lewis's journal in Douglas Southall Freeman, "George Washington"

MRS. CARROLL'S ICED SANGAREE

    2 peach stones
    1 orange, sliced and seeded
    ¼ cup sugar
    1 lemon, sliced and seeded
    1 cup brandy
    10 strawberries
    2 ripe peaches, sliced
    2 nectarine stones
    2 slices fresh pineapple cubed or crushed
    1 bottle claret wine
    2 ripe nectarines
    2 cups club soda

Crack peach stones and take out kernels. Add sugar and brandy to the fruit, nectarine stones, and peach kernels and let stand for several hours in the bottom of punch bowl. When ready to serve, remove nectarine stones and peach kernels and pour claret and club soda into bowl. Add an ice ring made with fresh peach leaves or sprigs of fresh mint. Add a portion of fruit to each cup.

Francis Scott Key, *who brought lasting fame to Ft. McHenry, was born in Frederick County in 1779.*

When the British fleet was readying for the attack, Key heard that his friend Dr. Beanes, was being held on one of the British ships and went to the British Admiral to plead for the Doctor's release. His request was finally granted, but both men were told they must remain on the flagship until Baltimore was taken. So began the bombardment, which continued for hours all through the night. It was not until the dawn that Key saw, with great relief "Our flag was still there". He was so deeply moved by the sight, he wrote the poem, which has become the much loved national anthem **"The Star Spangled Banner".** *It first appeared in print on the day after the battle, as a broadside from the "Baltimore American and Commercial Advertiser" printed by a 14 year old lad, Samuel Sands, under the title "Defence of Ft. McHenry". It was put to the music of a popular tavern song of the day, and performed at the theatre a few weeks later.*

It is a tradition which has survived from the early 18th century (circa 1730) to serve this heart-warming drink during the hard winters. It was also supposed to have warmed the cockles of the North Point troops hearts before the victorious battle in 1814.

The recipe for **FISH HOUSE PUNCH**

> *One pint lemon juice, three pints mixes, viz:*
> *one pint Jamaica rum, one pint brandy, one pint peach brandy; four pounds sugar and nine pints water. Make Lemonade first, then add liquors, stir — and jump back!*

Should you make this and taste it, you'll know why the troops were victorious and the British were routed.

A TOAST

"To woman's love — to man's not akin,
   For her heart is a home,
      while his heart is an 'inn'."

COLONIAL RECIPES
BOMBERGER

Star Spangled Banner Flag House 1793. Mary Pickersgill's home. She sewed the flag of 15 stars and 15 stripes which inspired Francis Scott Key to write the "Star Spangled Banner" during the Battle of Baltimore in 1814.

ROSE BRANDY

Fill a large bottle with damask rose petals, picked while they are fresh; fill the bottle with brandy, or good spirits of any kind; cork it tightly and set it away for use. It will bear filling up several times.

DOMESTIC COOKERY
BY ELIZABETH E. LEA
BALTIMORE 1853. Cushing & Bailey

A **TOAST** from William Makepeace Thackeray,

"I drink it as the Fates ordain it,
come, fill it and have done with rhymes;
Fill up the lonely glass and drain it
In memory of dear old times."

BLACKBERRY CORDIAL

Mash and strain blackberries; put the juices on to boil in a brass or bell-metal kettle; skim it well, and to each gallon of juice put three pounds of sugar and a quart of spirits; bruise some cloves and put in. This is valuable as a medicine for children in summer.

DOMESTIC COOKERY
BY ELIZABETH E. LEA
BALTIMORE 1853. Cushing & Bailey

KALTE ENTE is a traditional German cold punch. It is a refreshing form of fruit cup.
It needs slices of fresh lemon which have been sugared.

> 1 part dry sparkling wine
> 2 parts dry Moselle or Rhine wine
> Pour the wines over lemon
> slices in serving bowl or
> large jug. Chill and serve

There are many variations, half soda water and sparkling wine: claret in place of moselle: other fresh fruits such as stawberries and peaches or a glass of Curacao.

A cure for coughs —

DR PHYSICKS COUGH PILLS

> *Gum ammonia — 1 dram*
> *Powdered squills — 30 grains*
> *Powdered opium — 8 grains*
> *Castile soap — 4 grains*

Mix and divide into 30 pills. Take one, morning, noon and night.

Part of the roof line of a row of houses near Fort McHenry.

Close by the Mount Clare Mansion is the 2600 block of Wilkens Avenue which is the longest unbroken block of row houses in the city and an example of Baltimore's famous white marble steps.

ALE CUP

Cut two small lemons into thin slivers, remove
any pips. Take 1 teacupful of sherry and 1 pint
of dark brown ale 1 teaspoon nutmeg, pour over
lemon slivers: mix thoroughly, ice and serve.

WINE SPICED BROTH

1 cup fresh orange juice
2 cups water
2 cups dry white wine
4 tablespoons honey
½ teaspoon salt
3 tablespoons lemon juice
2 cinnamon sticks
2 tablespoons flour
6 egg whites (or 1 pint heavy cream)
½ teaspoon nutmeg
½ teaspoon ginger powder

Place first six ingredients into saucepan and simmer gently for 3 minutes. Remove ½ cup of broth and stir flour into it. Stir flour mixture into broth and simmer for a further 4 minutes stirring while the mixture thickens slightly. Remove cinnamon sticks. Next blend the nutmeg and ginger with the egg white or with the whipping cream and whip until the mixture forms peaks. Pour the "potage" or broth into individual tankards or bowls and garnish just before serving with a large dollop of spiced meringue or cream. You have a choice of serving this "Wyne Potage" as a soup or a drink!

9 North Front Street

"The beautiful Maryland marble which graced so many Baltimore homes and buildings, was sent far and wide. There is Maryland marble used in the wonderful Taj Mahal in India.

Miss A. Pue's Recipe

"FOR REMOVING STAINS FROM MARBLE

Have compounded at the apothecary; Two ounces common soda. 1 ounce pumice stone. 1 ounce fine powdered chalk. Sift through fine seive and mix with water. Rub mixture well, all over the marble and the stains will be removed by rubbing it with lemon juice."

MULLED PEAR CIDER
    2 quarts fresh pear juice
    ¼ teaspoon nutmeg
    1/8 teaspoon thyme
    ½ teaspoon ginger powder
    7 sticks of cinnamon
    Sprinkle of sweet basil

Gently simmer the juice with all the spices except the basil. Break the cinnamon sticks and place some in each glass or tankard. Pour the warmed juice over the cinnamon stick in each glass, add a light sprinkle of basil on top and serve.

SPICY POMEGRANATE DRINK
    1½ cups water
    1 cup sugar
    ½ teaspoon cinnamon
    ¼ teaspoon nutmeg
    1/8 teaspoon ginger
    4 whole cloves
    ½ lemon
    1 quart fresh pomegranate juice
    (6-8 medium sized pomegranates,
    skinned pith removed, seeds
    removed pulverized and strained).

Use a large enamel pot and combining water, sugar and spices, bring to boil and gently simmer for 7 minutes. Take out whole cloves. Grate finely the rind of the lemon and put to one side, squeeze the ½ lemon and add lemon juice to pomegranate juice and combine with spiced hot fluid. Slowly bring to the boil and simmer for 2 minutes. Serve warm with a garnish of grated lemon peel for each glass. Or serve cool with a garnish of lemon slice on each glass.

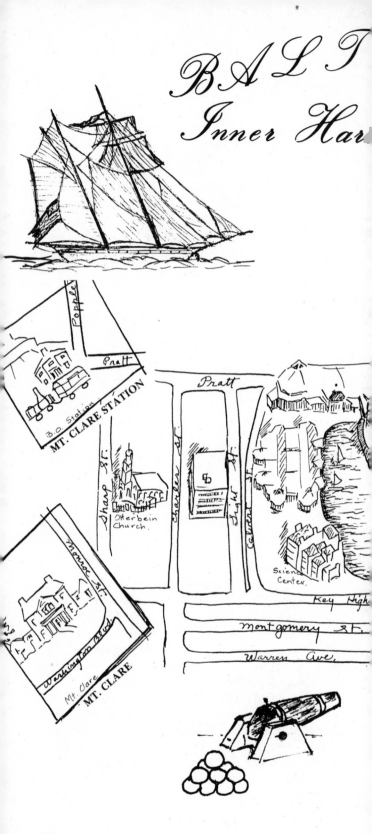

BALT

Inner Har

Pratt

Poppl

MT. CLARE STATION

B.O. Station

Pratt

Sharp St.

Charles St.

Light St.

Calvert

Otterbein
Church.

Science
Center.

Monroe St.

Washington Blvd

Mt Clare

MT. CLARE

Key High

Montgomery St.

Warren Ave.

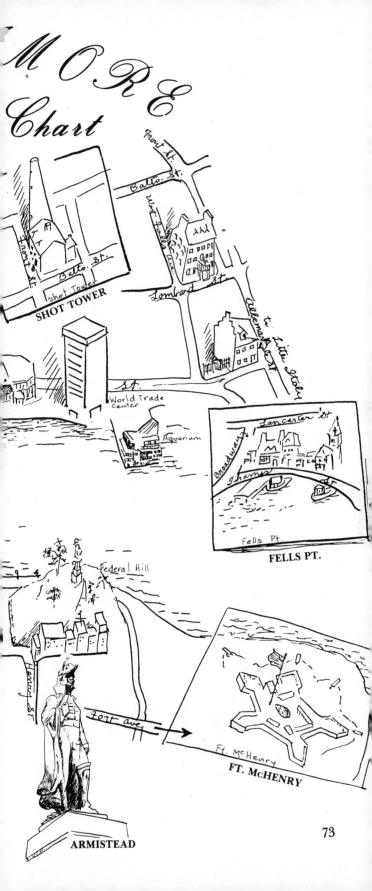

MORE
Chart

SHOT TOWER

World Trade Center

Aquarium

FELLS PT.

Federal Hill

Fort ave.

FT. McHENRY

ARMISTEAD

73

Eliza Acton was a much respected and often quoted cook of the 19th century. Indeed, it was she who first separated the ingredients from the method, in her recipe books. Her recipe for **OXFORD BISHOP** is a delicious, warming Yuletide drink.

Make several cuts in the rind of a lemon, stick cloves in the cuts and roast the lemon by a slow fire. Put ¼ teaspoon each of cinnamon cloves, mace and allspice, with a pinch of ginger into an enamel suacepan with half a pint of water; boil until it is reduced one half. Boil one bottle of port wine, reduce some of the spirit by applying a lighted taper to the saucepan; put the roasted lemon and spice mixture into the wine, stir well and stand by the fire for ten minutes. Rub a few cubes of sugar on the rind of a fresh lemon to absorb the zest, place sugar in serving bowl (warmed) or a cube in each tankard, pour the wine into it, grate in some nutmeg. When serving in punchbowl leave the lemon and spices floating in it.

Finally a **WARMING CUP** for the festive season.

    4 quarts of full cream milk
    Rind of 6 lemons
    2 eggs
    ¼ pint of cold milk
    1 pint Jamaica Rum
    ½ pink brandy
    4 ozs castor sugar
    Grated nutmeg

Carefully pare lemons leaving out the white pith. Place rum, brandy and sugar with lemon peel in a sealed jar for two days, shake a few times to dissolve sugar.

When you are ready to make the punch, beat two eggs with ¼ pint of cold milk. Bring the 2 quarts of milk to boiling with the lemon rind from the jar. In another pan warm the liquid from the jar. Remove rind from milk — whisk in beaten eggs add warmed liquid. Grate a little nutmeg on top. Serve in warmed glasses. The punch should be served warm not hot.

Good broth and good keeping
do much now and then.
Good diet with wisdom
best comforteth man.

17th century.

Maritime records reveal that the first Baltimore clipper ship was built in 1810 at a shipyard on Phillpott Street.

The clippers were built to beat the blockade of the British. Their speed earned them an enviable reputation and saved many a man from impressment into the British Navy.

The "Ann McKim" was a Baltimore Clipper of 1830, built for the China trade, a trip that took about 90 days.

There was another Clipper built in Baltimore, the China Clipper built by the Glenn L. Martin Company in 1935, at Middle River. It was flown to Manila in 5 days. That Clipper has also made way for the new. A hundred years hence who can predict what the "Baltimore Clipper" will be? Perhaps the most modern space ship for inter-stellar travel!

Bride of Baltimore